The
Secrets
of
Tropical Rainforests

HOT AND HUMID AND TEEMING WITH LIFE

BY JEAN HAMILTON

LONDON TOWN PRESS

Jean-Michel Cousteau *presents*

Jean-Michel Cousteau
Publishing Director

Series Editor
Vicki León

The Secrets of Tropical Rainforests
Principal photographers
Kevin Schafer, Martha Hill, and Michael Fogden

Additional photographers
Frank Balthis; Hans and Judy Beste; John Cancalosi; John Chellman; Earth Scenes; E.R. Degginger; Michael Fogden; François Gohier; Martha Hill; Steven Holt; Breck P. Kent; Frans Lanting; Richard K. LaVal; Wayne Lynch; Kevin Schafer; Dr. Nigel Smith; Larry Ulrich; Doug Wechsler; Belinda Wright

London Town Press
P.O. Box 585
Montrose, California 91021
www.LondonTownPress.com

Book design by Christy Hale
10   9   8   7   6   5   4   3   2

Printed in Singapore

Distributed by Publishers Group West

Publisher's Cataloging-in-Publication Data
Hamilton, Jean.
The secrets of tropical rainforests : hot and humid and teeming with life / Jean Hamilton ; photographs by Kevin Schafer [et al.] —2nd ed.
p.   cm. — (London Town wild life series)
Originally published: San Luis Obispo, CA : Blake Books ©1993
Summary: Explores the rich animal and plant life found within the layers of a tropical rainforest, and discusses the consequences of deforestation locally and globally.
Includes bibliographic references and index.
ISBN 978-0-9666490-5-5
1. Rain forest ecology—Juvenile literature.   2. Rain forests—Juvenile literature. 3. Rain forest animals —Juvenile literature.
[1. Rain forest ecology. 2. Rain forests.] I. Schafer, Kevin. II. Title. III. Series.
QH541.5.R27 H36 2005
577.34—dc22
2004117674

FRONT COVER: A sifaka from Madagascar, one of the endangered monkeys on that African island.

TITLE PAGE: A glasswing butterfly in South America often escapes detection, thanks to its see-through wings.

BACK COVER: The toucans of the Amazon rainforest love fruit pulp and berries of all kinds.

Contents

A Garden of Eden worth saving

Our world was once an emerald paradise of tropical rainforests almost pole to pole. Scientists have found fossilized pollen from rainforest plants in such unlikely places as London, Alaska, and Tennessee.

When the first Ice Age arrived, rainforests retreated toward the equator. That green belt shrank and expanded as the Ice Ages came and went. Until modern times, the rainforest occupied much land on either side of the equator. Today, however, satellite photos show the rainforest belt in tatters, burnt and cut into patches that get smaller every day.

Latin America holds over half the remaining rainforest, mostly in the Amazon and Orinoco river basins of Brazil and Venezuela. Another 25% is left in the Asian tropics. The rest survives, poorly protected, in Central and West Africa, with isolated patches in Australia, India, and on islands like Madagascar and Borneo.

These ancient forests cover less than 6% of the land on our planet, yet may contain 30 million different species of living things.

Such large ecosystems are called biomes, and the rainforest biome includes several types. Cloud rainforests, found at higher altitudes, are usually bathed in fog. Mangrove rainforests are located where the sea meets the land. Rainforests further from the equator have wet and dry seasons.

True tropical rainforests, also called lowland or equatorial rainforests, are hot, humid, and wet. Temperatures average 80 degrees Fahrenheit year-round. Eighty to 400 inches of rain fall evenly throughout the year. These rainforests teem with evergreen trees, other plants, and animal life on four levels: floor, understory, canopy, and pavilion. This stable environment is the greatest and greenest in nature.

◄ Rainforests are the wettest ecosystems on dry land. This fern-filled forest in Hawaii has waterfalls. Other rainforests often contain rivers, flooded areas, and swamps.

▲ In South America, caimans like this one swim and hunt in river-filled rainforests. Caimans are related to the crocodiles of Australia, Asia, Cuba, and Africa, and the alligators of China and North America.

Most of the rainforest plant life relies on sunlight. When sun hits the green chlorophyll in leaves, it produces carbohydrates the plants use for energy. This magic feat is called photosynthesis.

Five groups of vegetation live in the rainforest. First are the giants, the hardwood trees like teak, mahogany, and rosewood. Called climax trees, these slow growers tower above the lighter, flimsier trees that pioneer growth, like balsa and tree ferns. Rainforest climax trees tend to grow straight and tall before putting out a green "roof" of branches and leaves.

Like climax trees, members of the next three groups—climbers, stranglers, and epiphytes—also make their own food, but need supports on which to grow.

Climbers use hooks, suckers, corkscrews, and bristles to claw their way upward. The most familiar climber is the liana vine of Tarzan fame. Lianas grow hundreds of feet long, often outliving many of the trees that support them.

▶ The hoatzin, a bird of the Amazon, is related to the cuckoo but resembles the archaeopteryx, the earliest known bird, which came on the scene about 100 million years ago.

Climbers use trees as trellises, twisting their way up. There they form a network of woody loops and links across the canopy, a highway for creatures in the upper stories. Climbers often link trees together at the top. That may cause one tree to pull down others in high winds.

Stranglers twine around trees for support, often killing their host. The most common stranglers belong to the fig family. A strangler fig begins as an air plant sprouting on a branch from a seed dropped by a bird or bat. Aerial roots creep to the forest floor, dig in, then climb back toward the sunlight. In time, the roots of one or more stranglers form a living coffin around its now-dead host. In turn, the strangler and its fruits become bed and breakfast for many other life forms.

Epiphytes (nicknamed "air plants") make their homes on bark and high branches. Unlike stranglers, they don't harm trees. Epiphytes thrive on a diet of sunlight and moisture. Once established, they also collect soil particles from the air. Over time, these particles become thick humus, piling up at

◄ Plants compete for space and light in rainforests. Sunlight turns the chlorophyll in leaves into energy the plants can use. On the shady forest floor, leaves grow big to capture the feeble sunlight, providing lots of good hiding places for hunters like snakes.

▲ At 100 pounds or more, the capybara is the largest rodent in the world. It forages on land but is happiest in the water, which keeps it from getting sunburnt.

the base of bigger branches. Many epiphytes are ferns, mosses, and other non-flowering plants. Mosses knit together bits of soil, making a canopy mat that the tree host can use as well.

Bromeliads and orchids are the flashy epiphytes. Bromeliads dominate the canopies of cooler cloud rainforests in Central America. Their cuplike centers often form ponds, home to other canopy dwellers. Orchids flourish at different heights, including on fallen logs. Over a hundred species of orchids have been identified on a single tree.

Last are saprophytes or molds and fungi, including mushrooms. They have no chlorophyll; instead they feed on rotting material. Along with insects, they're the cleanup crew of the floor. Over 2,000 parasites also dwell here—including rafflesia, the world's largest flower. Like an alien, this 25-pound monster springs from a woody vine, the stench of its orange-red bloom drawing flies.

An acre of rainforest may hold hundreds of plant and tree species. In fact, more than half the world's tree species have a rainforest address. Often as high as a 20-story skyscraper, these trees make mini- and micro-habitats at different levels.

▶ The heliconia flower uses its red color to attract hummingbirds and butterflies. Its shape exactly fits the curved bill of a certain hummer.

▲ Pink orchids like these often hitchhike on upper limbs of big trees. They are epiphytes or air plants.

They don't get this size because of rich soil. Instead, each tree is helped by tiny fungi. In return for sugars from the trees, fungi threads act as extensions of tree roots. That allows the tree to absorb more water and nutrients than it could on its own. This underground partnership is called mycorrhizae: Greek for "mushroom roots."

Big trees aren't the only ones getting help from unlikely places. Rainforests are remarkable for the number of plants and animals that form mutual partnerships. Examples of symbiosis or interdependence are everywhere.

For instance, the Brazil nut tree depends on one particular bee to pollinate it. When its pods ripen, only a large rodent called the agouti can open them. Then it has to crack the equally tough Brazil nuts inside. The agouti eats the oil-rich nuts and buries others for later. It forgets where some are hidden—and those few become new trees.

The vanilla orchid has high-climbing vines, white flowers, and seed pods with a heavenly scent. They attract certain bats, who nibble the pods and scatter the seeds throughout the forest. Without that bat, our world wouldn't have vanilla ice cream.

The stiff leaves of the bromeliad conceal

◄ These trees grow huge in poor soil. How? Their roots link up with helpful fungi. The woody, wing-like extensions from the tree's trunk are called buttresses.

▲ The South American howler monkey earns its name. This leaf-eater may be the loudest voice in the rainforest.

a busy water world: crab larvae, dragonfly nymphs that eat them, daddy-long-legs, jumping millipedes, tadpoles, woodlice, earwigs, and earthworms with brilliant blue noses. These creatures help each other and feed on each other. Their waste products nourish the bromeliad. In this way, each element raises the life expectancy of another element, and ultimately of the rainforest itself.

All plant and animal communities of the rainforest live on one of four levels: floor, understory, canopy, and pavilion.

The floor of the tropical rainforest

The rainforest floor is quite open, looking much the same whether in Latin America, Asia, Africa, or the Pacific Islands. Dead leaves and seeds drift down, joining the litter on the ground. Foliage cuts off the sun, making green shadows. Insects hum and drone. The air smells sweet and musky, of growth and decay.

Suddenly a raindrop falls; then another. In minutes, clouds dump so much rain that the forest appears to be under a waterfall. Gradually, the drumming noise of a million raindrops comes to a stop—until the next shower. Rain may fall ten times a day.

Plants on the floor adapt to a life of shade and deprivation. Their leaves are often huge, to absorb what sun they receive. Ferns, shrubs, and saplings wait years for a large tree to fall. When it does, it makes a sunny gap in the gloom. Only then can smaller plants begin an upward journey that may take a century.

The soil is surprisingly poor and thin. Trees send out shallow roots, leaving few nutrients in the topsoil. Termites break down leaf litter before it has a chance to enrich the soil. Animal droppings and carcasses that would fertilize the earth in a temperate forest are quickly claimed by other insects, especially beetles.

Male beetles of the Canthon species particularly like monkey dung, slicing off pieces with their hind legs. A female dung beetle selects her mate by the size of his dung ball, which she scrambles onto as the male rolls it. They mate, depositing the eggs on the dung ball. Then they bury the prize which later feeds their brood.

Insects from bees to butterflies are everywhere. But none outnumber the termites and ants.

Termite nests begin below ground, like parking garages. They often rise into mounds

◄ Termites make multi-story nests like this one out of mud and saliva.

◄ Insects work hard recycling on the rainforest floor. A pooper scooper, the dung beetle cleans up and wins a mate at the same time.

many feet high. A single acre may hold a thousand nests or termitaries, each jammed with up to ten million insects. One million termites can eat up to twelve tons of wood each year. Without them, the rainforest would soon disappear under its own litter.

A new termitary gets its start with the flight of thousands of large winged termites. One female drops to the ground, discards her wings, and signals any male who survived the flight that she's ready to set up housekeeping.

A termite queen lays 5,000 eggs a day for 15 years or so. When she gets too fat to leave her chamber, the queen stops work—and the workers promptly kill her.

Ant populations are equally huge. Colonies of leafcutter ants may contain millions. These hard-working farmers use leaves as compost, growing fungi to feed the colony. With jaws like scissors, they slice leaves into chunks and hold them like banners, making a non-stop parade back to the nest.

Army ants have no permanent nest. Like their cousins, the driver ants of Africa, they set up new camps each night. Soldiers link together to form a living nest. Inside it, nurse ants tend the queen and the young, called larvae. At dawn, the soldiers stream

▶ Army ants, famous and feared, follow scent trails to food along the rainforest floor.

out and attack everything in their path, tearing prey with huge pincers and carrying it back to camp. For two weeks, this raiding and camping continues. When the larvae begin to spin cocoons, the colony settles down for several weeks, while the queen lays eggs for new larvae. Meanwhile, new worker ants emerge from the cocoons.

In a couple of days, the colony returns to roaming. Little stops these restless insects. Army ants cross streams by hooking their legs to form a living bridge or raft. Only wildfire and wide rivers can halt their progress.

Other creatures of the rainforest floor come out at night, or rely on camouflage or mimicry. Look at a vine long enough, and it may wiggle away, becoming an emerald tree boa. A walking stick insect imitates a twig. A pile of leaves conceals the snaky coils of a poisonous fer-de-lance. Even a piece of tree bark may take flight, becoming a blue morpho butterfly.

▶ Among army ants, the soldiers have large heads and huge jaws, called mandibles. Human doctors sometimes use ant mandibles to hold together the wounds of injured people.

Some animals are less shy. In a clearing, you might come upon cocks-of-the-rock, busy parading for females in a courtship area called a lek. Male birds continue their displays as long as hens appear, advertising themselves with bright orange colors.

In Asian rainforests, junglefowl are the flashy ones. If they look like chickens, there's a reason. These glossy birds are the ancestral stock of our hens and roosters.

The giant anteater also lives on the floor. Its curved claws demolish termites' nests, no matter how tall. With the barbs on its

▶ Some birds use the rainforest floor to show off to females, like this bright orange male, called the cock-of-the-rock.

sticky, 24-inch tongue, it can lick up insects faster than you can devour a popsicle.

Rainforest plants and animals have adapted to survive extreme conditions. If you could fly above the Amazon River, you'd see it winding through the rainforest like a giant brown snake. Each year, the river floods. Some areas remain underwater for six months or even year-round. For that reason, many land creatures are quite at home in the water.

The jaguar is one. The New World's largest cat, it goes after pig-like peccaries that root in mud, chasing them into the river for a sunset kill. The plump tapir, with its hose-like nose, is a favorite prey. The jaguar needs to catch the tapir on land, however, because the tapir is actually a better swimmer. At times, the jaguar goes fishing. Using its tail as bait, it snags catfish for dinner.

In muddy pools lurks the massive anaconda. It waits for prey like the capybara, largest of all rodents, to come and drink. The larger green anaconda can even bring down a jaguar, squeezing it to death in its huge coils.

In flooded areas along river banks, the hoatzin bird builds its tree nest. If alarmed, its chicks drop into the water and swim into tangled vegetation. The young have two claws near each wing tip, useful for climbing back into the nest.

▲ The tapir is a loner, a night feeder that prefers thick jungle next to the river. It roots for plants in South American and Asian rainforests. In Africa, its nearest relative is the forest hog.

Although the six-foot-long giant otter of South America swims expertly and fishes for a living, it stays by shallow water, like the oxbow lakes in the Amazon.

Even the sloth swims when the Amazon floods. The trees it lives in remain partly underwater for months. During this time, river fishes change their diet, swimming up to trees and eating fruit right off them. In flood season, some insects stay put and get wet; others migrate upward in the trees.

Just as many land creatures are at home in the water, many river creatures are at home on land. These include crocodiles, yapoks (the only aquatic marsupial), and leeches. Strangest of all is the lungfish, which can gulp air. Its ancestors adapted to stagnant lakes 350 million years ago.

▶ The timid anteater rarely confronts anything larger than an ant or termite. When it does, it assumes a defensive posture, as this Costa Rican collared anteater is doing. Its heavy claws break into nests so it can slurp up insects with its sticky tongue. Some anteater species even climb trees and have prehensile tails that grasp like hands.

The understory

► To help bats, birds, and others find them, some plants grow large fruits and flowers from their trunks and main branches. This adaptation is called cauliflory.

F rom the floor, the understory rises about 60 feet in the air. For creatures living here, the tangle of branches and vines lets them move about with ease.

Dozens of useful plants originally came from this shady level: coffee, cacao, lemon, cloves, avocado, lime, and banana trees among them. Since wet leaves are often attacked by fungi, many have pointed drip-tips, letting rain drain quickly.

In the understory, vivid flowers and fruit sometimes grow directly from tree trunks and main branches. More than a thousand species exhibit this adaptation, called cauliflory. The cacao tree, where we get chocolate, is one. Others are papaya and calabash gourd trees.

Some plants need bats or insects to pollinate them. Their flowers and fruit tend to have strong smells—not all of them pleasant to human noses.

Other understory plants produce colorful, juicy fruit. Fruit is a reward, the plant's way of making its seed attractive. If seeds drop near the parent plant, overcrowding will result. When fruit bats, birds, and animals take fruit, the seeds are also carried away in their digestive tracts for dispersal.

Originally, all New World bats ate insects. Now bats specialize. They may eat fruit, nectar, pollen, fish, lizards, mice, birds, frogs, or even other bats. Although vampire bats occur in rainforest regions, the blood they feed on is usually from a domestic cow or hog. Unlike in the movies, they rarely attack human beings.

◄ Bats like this Australian flying fox feast on fruit. By eating fruit, bats spread plant seeds far and wide. Plants depend on bats, birds, mammals, and butterflies to transfer pollen and seeds.

Red-eyed leaf frogs and other amphibians sing
together. Scientists have discovered that male frogs
form choruses, not to outcroak each other but
for safety in numbers. Bright as a jar of jellybeans,
the red-eyed leaf frog has sticky pads on fingers
and toes, letting it move easily in any direction.

Many bat species do good deeds. When they feed on nectar, they help plants reproduce by transferring pollen from one flowering plant to another. This is called pollination.

Over a thousand species of butterflies live in the rainforest, from understory to canopy. They're vital as pollen carriers too.

Understory animals tend to be small and lightweight, with grasping paws and long bushy tails, used for counterbalance. The coati, a raccoon relative, thrives in the understory. Coatis travel in bands of up to 40 animals, feeding on whatever they can catch, including frogs.

A tree frog is designed for understory life. Its toes have suction cups that secrete a sticky mucus, letting these frogs climb steep vertical surfaces. Here, too, we find geckos and chameleons. A chameleon clamps two toes on one side of a limb and three on the other, making for a sturdy grip.

Tree-dwelling reptiles and amphibians often give birth to live young rather than laying eggs. Tree species have fewer off-spring. The young, however, have more chance to survive because of the time they spend in the mother's body. Provided, of course, their mother doesn't become a meal for a coati.

The Amazon understory also shelters two small cats that hunt at different times of day, the ocelot and the margay. These elegant predators have coats that blend with dappled light. Margays hunt smaller rodents and lizards, while the larger ocelot will go after big rodents and even the pint-sized brocket deer.

▲ The cacao tree is an example of cauliflory. Inside its brown pods are cacao beans, where we get chocolate.

► Anole lizards live in the strangler fig but use the forest floor as a battleground. These two males puff up their bright throats, called dewlaps, displaying to win the attention of female lizards. Sometimes they draw the attention of lizard-loving birds.

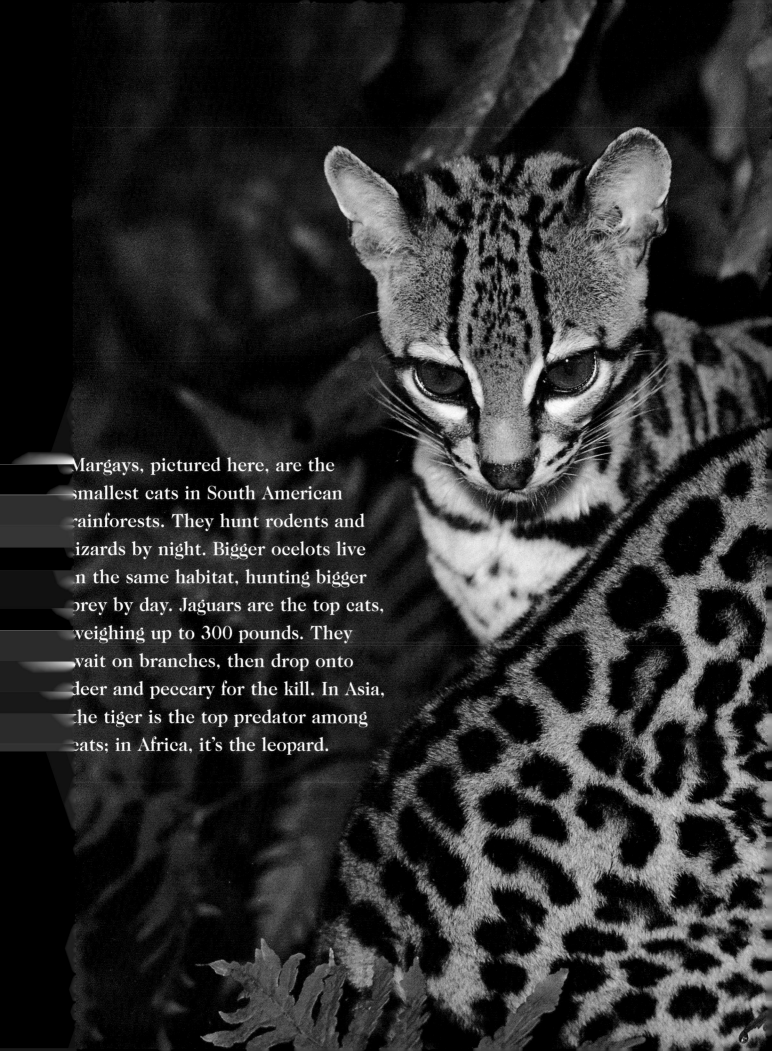

Margays, pictured here, are the smallest cats in South American rainforests. They hunt rodents and lizards by night. Bigger ocelots live in the same habitat, hunting bigger prey by day. Jaguars are the top cats, weighing up to 300 pounds. They wait on branches, then drop onto deer and peccary for the kill. In Asia, the tiger is the top predator among cats; in Africa, it's the leopard.

The canopy

The rainforest canopy begins about 60 feet up. As it rises to 120 feet or so, the climate changes. There is less humidity and more air movement and temperature variation.

In the canopy, creatures have room to fly, glide, or leap about in safety. This makes it a high traffic area for traveling animals. Some branches remain free of plants because they're used so much. Up to 90% of all plants and animals in a rainforest may live here.

To the creatures in it, the canopy is a sunlit paradise. The area of maximum flowering, it offers the most tender leaves and the

◄ Bromeliads like this lipstick-red plant grow high in the canopy. It's an epiphyte or air plant, living on a tree but taking nothing from it. Its water-filled center shelters small animals and plants. The poison-arrow frog, for instance, puts one of its tadpoles into each bromeliad pond to grow in safety.

▲ Some birds, like this red and blue eclectus parrot, feed and sleep in the canopy.

freshest fruit. In the Amazon, canopy trees flower at different times. But Asian rainforests have periodic mass flowerings, when petals from up to 100 different kinds of trees drift onto the forest floor, like confetti at a parade.

At this height, many trees also put forth "canopy roots" that find their way into the aerial gardens of epiphytes on their branches. Like tree roots underground, these link to helpful fungi.

Bird life is intense. Some species are large, loud, and spectacular, like parrots, macaws, and toucans. Others are silent hunters, like hawks and owls. Among the plant pollinators and nectar drinkers are hundreds of hummingbird species. Each year, these tiny birds migrate thousands of miles to winter in the rainforest. Many species of butterflies migrate here as well.

Parrots climb about the canopy with ease, foraging for seeds, fruits, and flowers. They feed, bathe, socialize, and rest in the treetops. Long popular for their beauty and intelligence, parrots and macaws are stalked by poachers worldwide. To make matters worse, when trees are cut down, these birds lose nesting areas.

Also endangered are canopy birds like the seldom-seen resplendent quetzal, which feeds on wild avocadoes in Guatemalan rainforests. On the other side of the world, the equally beautiful bird of paradise hides in the rainforests of Papua New Guinea.

◄ One-third of the world's bird species, including the blue and yellow macaw, either live in the rainforest or migrate long distances to it, to spend the winter.

► The tiny squirrel monkey feeds on fruit and insects. In the canopy, it often plays and forages in large groups, following bigger monkeys.

A toucan has a boat-shaped bill, light in weight but almost as long as its body. With it, it can flip fruits and berries into its mouth. Colored differently for each species, the bill is more than a feeding tool. In leafy forests, it helps each species spot its own kind and find a mate.

South American toucans resemble the hornbills of African and Asian rainforests. Both families have huge, bright bills and slender bodies. Both nest in tree cavities and feast on fruit pulp. But biologists have found they aren't closely related. They are good examples of "convergent evolution"—where, on different continents, two species evolve similar shapes and behaviors as a response to similar demands in their environment.

Canopy monkeys show how similar animals can coexist peacefully by occupying different levels. The howler monkey lives mostly in the upper reaches and has a sweet tooth for figs, plums, and the pulp in cacao pods. The spider monkey favors the middle layers, where it can find its favorite foods, wild nutmeg and bean-like nuts. Capuchins eat and live in the lower part of the canopy, sometimes descending to the understory and floor. The only monkey which feels free to eat on all three levels is the douroucouli, because it is active at night, when the others are asleep.

Each species claims territory by calling. The howler monkey drowns out the rest with its barking roars, the loudest made by any animal. In dense foliage, calling maintains contact. By vocalizing, troop members locate each other, point out food sources, and warn of danger.

The canopy's best acrobat, the spider monkey makes use of its long limbs and talented tail. Along with other species, the spider monkey has a prehensile or grasping tail, used as an extra hand.

In South American rainforests, monkeys aren't the only residents equipped with such tails. The raccoon-like kinkajou, the prehensile-tailed porcupine, and two kinds of arboreal or tree-dwelling anteaters also roam the treetops with extra tail-end assurance. In Asian rainforests, fewer creatures have prehensile tails; more species move between trees by gliding.

Lemurs, a group of big-eyed, furry monkeys called prosimians, live on the African island of Madagascar. Their powerful legs let them bound and jump through the canopy like gymnasts. Their bushy tails serve more for balance than for grasping.

Some primates use a hand-over-hand way of traveling called brachiation. Most graceful and spectacular are the gibbons that live in Asian rainforests. Highly endangered orangutans and African gorillas also use brachiation to move through the canopy. So do chimpanzees.

Almost all primates can travel for miles through the trees, cartwheeling from one branch to another, leaping wild and free as though they were weightless. Now and then, they fall. A primatologists' study of wild gibbons found that more than half of them had healed fractures from past tumbles.

Nothing could seem more different from a monkey than a sloth. Greenish algae live in its shaggy fur, letting the sloth blend into the forest. Beetles and moths find its fur cozy, too. The sloth has long curved claws, handy for scratching those pests. Hanging upside down from a branch, the sloth eats, breeds, and raises young. It is famous for sleeping, without moving, for up to 18 hours at a time. Its diet of tender leaves takes 100 hours to digest. In fact, this slow-poke has a metabolism so low that it needs to sunbathe to maintain its body heat.

▶A molasses-slow native of the canopy, the 3-toed sloth lives in a tree and does no more than it has to. Green algae, beetles and moths make homes in its fur. Once each week, the sloth travels to the base of its tree to relieve itself. While on the ground, moths fly out of its coat and lay eggs on the dung. Later, a new generation of moths will flutter up to the canopy to find homes on other sloths.

As the tallest trees emerge from the canopy, their leafy crowns form the pavilion, or "emergent layer." From 120 to 200 feet high, the crowns are the borderland between forest and sky—a place of strong winds, stinging rainshowers, and burning tropical sun.

Flying insects populate the pavilion. Whippoorwills and other birds that capture insects on the fly find the pavilion a prime feeding area. Hordes of mosquitoes hover, including ones that carry malaria and

◄ TOP: Birds and insects like katydids live in the pavilion. The katydid relies on color to protect itself. MIDDLE: When a spider gets hungry, katydid disguises don't always work. BOTTOM: Some katydids wear armor and spikes to keep from becoming a mouthful.

yellow fever. Whenever a tree falls, mosquitoes come down with it to feast on lower-story animals.

The Amazonian turkey vulture floats on updrafts above the trees, using its keen sense of smell to detect carrion or dead meat far below. Once it locates a meal, the vulture hops its way down to the floor. Other vultures may join the feast but don't squabble the way that African vultures do. The turkey vulture dines slowly until forced to give way to the larger king vulture.

Because its sense of smell is poor, the king vulture lets the turkey vulture lead it to a carcass. With its stronger beak, the

▲ High in the pavilion, the king vulture reigns. Instead of hunting, it waits until the turkey vulture has found a dead animal. Then it descends to eat first.

37

king vulture then rips open the tough skin that the smaller bird cannot manage. When the king has finished, the turkey vultures return to feed.

Top predator of the pavilion is the harpy, largest and most powerful of eagles. The female harpy outweighs her mate. This bird has feet as big as a full-grown man's, armed with sharp talons, and a stare that would scare King Kong. Its wings are short and rounded for flying through forests. A harpy can chase a monkey through the canopy at 50 miles per hour, or carry off a full-grown sloth and its baby.

Harpies build huge, messy nests, and together raise the young. Two eggs are laid. When the first chick hatches, the second is ignored. If it does hatch, it's usually pecked to death by the first. The second egg seems to be for insurance, a survival tactic used by other birds.

Few reptiles or amphibians brave the heights of the pavilion. They can't generate their own heat, so these cold-blooded animals prefer the warmth of lower levels. One exception is the flying gecko. Instead of flying, this leaping lizard glides, using webbed toes and flaps of skin along its legs, sides, and tail. As it soars from tree to tree, its flaps open like a colorful parachute.

◀ From time to time, the pavilion treetops explode with color. Pink, yellow, and cream flowers fall to the ground, a perfumed feast for deer, lizards, and others.

A Garden of Eden
we can save

► Forest dwellers know their environment well. As youngsters, native people learn which plants to use as food or medicines, and which to avoid.

I n the 19th century, naturalists had to content themselves with exploring the rainforest at ground level. Most attempts to study the upper levels failed. Birds and mammals were shot, stuffed, and studied, but little was learned about their behavior.

Early in the 20th century, a British explorer named Hingston built the first observation platform in a Guiana forest. Platforms by others followed. These efforts allowed closer study of the rainforest, but of a limited area. In 1970, U.S. Army engineers designed a platform in Malaysia with connecting catwalks. With this rig, scientists could study a larger area, but the extensive structure changed animal behavior patterns.

◄ The Madagascar periwinkle flower, pictured with children from that island, fights diabetes, cancer, and children's leukemia. Other plants may offer even better medicine—but only if the rainforest survives.

Soon, however, a breakthrough occurred. Biologist Dr. Donald Perry pioneered an aerial network of ropes, opening up an area of Costa Rican rainforest from ground to pavilion. Now researchers could spend time in the canopy with minimum stress on the creatures being studied.

Today's scientists access the canopy in many ways. Some use hot-air balloons. One project used a blimp to lower an air-filled raft onto the canopy. Other sites use low-impact aerial walkways, platforms, and treehouses. Some biologists work from canopy cranes. Others prefer low-tech methods, like simple booms. Or they climb trees, using crossbows to send ropes over branches. Researchers work with an array of slings, harnesses, and pulleys that would astound the first rainforest explorers.

Longterm field research carried out by pioneering scientists like Perry, Margaret Lowman, Nalini Nadkarni, Robin Foster, and Louise Emmons has given us priceless information. Through them and others, we now know that orangutans, once thought of as solitary creatures, gather and socialize when certain fruit ripens in the canopy. We've learned of miniature "gardens of Eden" on high, plants collected and farmed by ants.

But time is running out. For years, big companies have looked at rainforests and seen only profit. They log the hardwood trees and burn the rest. They mine for gold and drill for oil. They clear land for cattle so that the world can have cheap hamburgers.

Each year we lose an area of rainforest the size of New York state. In 2003 alone, nearly six million acres of Amazonian rainforest were burned or cut down.

Biologists warn that rainforests aren't like other ecosystems. Once destroyed, this mighty yet fragile biome would be gone forever. Untold species of animals and plants would vanish,

and millions of people—most of them indigenous—would lose the place they call home.

Deforestation could also spell disaster for world climate. When rainforests are set afire, huge amounts of carbon dioxide are released into the air. Along with fossil fuels, this burning adds to global warming.

Governments everywhere have been slow to act. But dedicated people are hard at work, saving the rainforest in a variety of ways.

In the field, thousands of scientists work to catalog what's there, and how it interacts with everything else. Often they work through global helping organizations like Earthwatch, Flora & Fauna International, and Conservation International. Or, they work through universities and centers like the Smithsonian Tropical Research Institute. Other rainforest activists are ordinary folks, from schoolchildren to educators and seniors: people who cherish the wilderness, and act to save it.

Good things have been accomplished. Environmental groups have established wildlife sanctuaries. Governments have set

◄ Sustainable crops like iguana meat help indigenous people and their cultures survive without leaving their rainforest home.

aside rainforest for parks. In a dozen tropical nations, scientists have trained locals as naturalists. In dozens more, conservancy groups have protected rainforests through land purchase and debt-for-nature swaps. Songbird lovers have united with caffeine lovers to promote shade-grown coffee from understory trees, a critical winter habitat for millions of migrating birds.

Income from ecotourism has helped somewhat. It's now feasible to hike through rainforests, travel the Amazon by boat, even eavesdrop on canopy creatures from a Costa Rican aerial tram founded by Dr. Perry.

But the most important progress has come from the original inhabitants of the rainforest. From the islanders of Melanesia to the Indian tribes of Brazil, indigenous people have demanded more say. Their communities have taken economic control of rainforests. They've set up extractive reserves, where forest dwellers are legally allowed to harvest natural products from rubber to nuts to butterflies. And they're making a success of it.

That's not surprising. For centuries, rainforest people have harvested fruits, woods, medicines, and natural resins like shellac without damaging trees or destroying the ecosystem.

By protecting and managing resources in a sustainable way, forest dwelling communities preserve their rainforest home and maintain its biodiversity. Community forestry, as it's called, has another plus. It offers a hopeful path for millions of people to escape poverty by taking a direct role in their own future.

To the animals, plants, and native people who live in or near them, tropical rainforests are still paradise. To the rest of us, these forests hold the key to new medicines, food, and raw materials. Everything on our planet is linked, from the rainforests to us. The rainforest is our own backyard, and it is up to us to save it.

Rainforest secrets

- Jaguars hunt prey from tapirs to turtles. They even fish for piranha. When jaguars use their tails as "bait," sometimes the piranha fish bites off the tip!

- The rainforest is home to the biggest snake in the world—the green anaconda, up to 30 feet long. It's also home to the most poisonous snake, the fer-de-lance.

- Rainforests specialize in super-sized creatures. The Goliath beetle, world's biggest, has a wingspan of one foot. So does the Queen Alexandra birdwing butterfly. One rainforest bat has a five-foot wingspan.

- Rafflesia, the world's biggest flower, can weigh 25 pounds and have fleshy petals three feet wide. Some people also call it the world's stinkiest flower.

- The Cuban bee hummingbird, the world's smallest, lives high in the Cuban rainforest.

- We get lots of caffeine from the rainforest. Besides coffee beans, the forest gives us cacao (where we get chocolate), and kola nuts—the main ingredient of cola drinks.

- The water lily, the world's oldest flower, grows on Amazon rivers. Its lily pad is six feet wide—roomy enough to sit on.

- The spider monkey can support its entire weight hanging from its tail. Its clever tail can even hold a piece of fruit.

▼ Rainforest frogs like this one have long sticky fingers; special mucus lets them hold on to anything and travel in any direction.

Glossary

Biome. A large, complex ecosystem whose plants and animals live in a well-defined climate, like the rainforest.

Brachiation. To travel from tree branch to tree branch by swinging hand over hand. This way of moving is used by the gibbon, orangutan, gorilla, and chimpanzee. Humans can also brachiate.

Cauliflory. The growth of fruit or flowers directly from the trunk or main branches of a tree or plant.

Deforestation. The widespread cutting down of trees within forests ("clear-cutting"), especially old-growth trees.

Ecosystem. A stable community of plants, animals, and soil where nature is in balance.

Epiphyte. A plant without roots that makes its home on branches in rainforest trees. It gets its food and water from the air.

Extractive reserves. Places within rainforests where native peoples are legally allowed to harvest natural products, such as chicle, rubber, and cacao.

Forage. To feed or hunt.

Fungus (plural: fungi). A saprophyte or plant without chlorophyll that feeds on rotting material. Mushrooms, molds, and mildews are all fungi.

Indigenous. Original inhabitants of a given area.

Lek. An area, usually a clearing on the rainforest floor, where male birds compete and court females. Hummingbirds and cock-of-the-rock birds display in leks.

Mycorrhizae. An underground partnership between trees and fungi that helps both survive. Fungi bring nutrients from afar to tree roots, and receive sugars from the tree in return.

Oxbow lake. A U-shaped lake, formed from an old river.

Parasite. A plant or animal that lives off a host plant or animal, and often kills the host.

Pollen. Tiny yellow grains comprised of the male reproductive cells of flowers. When pollen links with the stigma of a flower, where the female cells are, fertilization takes place and the plant can reproduce.

Pollinators. In the rainforest, butterflies, birds, bats, and other creatures are pollinators that transfer pollen from one plant to another.

Predator. An animal that hunts others for food.

Prehensile. Flexible tail, often used as a fifth hand by certain monkeys and other rainforest animals.

Prey. An animal that is hunted for food by a predator.

Prosimian. A group of big-eyed monkeys, active at night, such as lemurs and bush babies.

Symbiosis. Interdependence or mutually helpful partnerships between plants and animals, or between two or more animals.

Termitaries. The large nests made by termites.

About the author

Science writer **Jean Hamilton** is also an award-winning novelist living on California's central coast.

Photographers

The work of 19 wonderful wildlife photographers graces these pages. Principal photographers were Michael Fogden, Kevin Schafer, and Martha Hill. The cover photo of a sifaka from Madagascar is by Frans Lanting. The back cover shot of a toucan came from John Chellman.

Frank Balthis, p. 11 top; Hans and Judy Beste/Animals Animals, p. 22; John Cancalosi/DRK photo, pp 32 left, 41; John Chellman/Animals Animals, back cover; Earth Scenes/Oxford Scientific Films, p. 26; E.R. Degginger/Animals Animals, p. 14; Michael Fogden/DRK photo, pp 1, 8-9, 24-25, 27, 30-31, 44; Michael Fogden/Animals Animals, p. 36 middle; Francois Gohier, pp 18, 33; Steven Holt/VIREO, pp 8 inset, 17 inset; Breck P. Kent/Animals Animals, p. 42 right; Frans Lanting/Minden Pictures, front cover, pp 6, 11 bottom, 38, 40; Richard K. LaVal, pp 20-21; Wayne Lynch/DRK Photo, p. 19; Kevin Schafer, pp 15, 28-29, 35, 37, 42 left; Kevin Schafer & Martha Hill, pp 7, 10, 13; Dr. Nigel Smith/Animals Animals, p. 32 right; Larry Ulrich/DRK Photo, p. 4; Doug Wechsler/VIREO, pp 12, 16-17, 23, 36 top, 36 bottom; Belinda Wright/DRK Photo, p. 43.

Special thanks

- Linda Countryman, docent for the Greater Los Angeles Zoo Association
- Janet Posen, Science Resource teacher for San Diego City schools
- David Loring, Southeast Asia Project Leader, Dietrick Institute for Applied Insect Ecology
- Thomas Ogren, science author and horticultural expert
- Noah Hawthorne, giant otter researcher, Tambopata Reserve, Peru
- Julie Dahlen, Children's Librarian, Paso Robles Public Library

MAP NOT TO SCALE

Where to see rainforests

- **Visit zoos with rainforest habitats.** Many of them let you walk through a habitat with tropical trees, plants, animals, butterflies, and birds. You'll see, hear, smell, and feel what a rainforest must be like.
- **Visit real rainforests,** from Costa Rica to Thailand to Hawaii. Money spent on local hotels, guides, food, and transport is a good way to encourage countries to save their rainforests instead of cutting them down. Some sites have aerial walkways or ropeways; one (in Costa Rica) has an aerial tram.
- **Armchair travel** through rainforests with videos, DVDs, and books. See our recommended list.
- **Eavesdrop on real expeditions** to the rainforest canopy in your classroom, through an online "electronic field trip" from The Jason Project (www.jasonproject.org). Developed by Dr. Robert Ballard (of "Raise the Titanic" fame), the Jason Project allows students around the world to see canopy research and other rainforest work in real time—and even ask questions of scientists. Get your school to sign up!
- **Go on actual scientific expeditions** to the rainforest through Earthwatch International (www.earthwatch.org). It has programs and scholarships for kids 16 and up; and teacher programs too.

Helping organizations & good websites

- Rainforest Action Network. Clear writing and great teacher and student resources, including Kid's Corner. Excellent fact sheets, especially the one on Medicinal Treasures of the Rainforest. www.ran.org
- Rainforest Alliance. Simple but information-packed website. This group certifies sustainable crops and products from farmers, foresters, and tour operators worldwide. www.rainforest-alliance.org
- World Rainforest Movement. The written materials of this well-organised activist group are a good mix of science and clear language: www.wrm.org.uy
- Earthwatch Institute, a science-based organization linking scientists with volunteers to carry out hundreds of fascinating research projects in more than 50 countries. The results provide solid data for conservation groups and sustainability efforts. www.earthwatch.org
- The Audubon Society does outstanding work on a number of topics, from bird counts to advocacy for rainforest